From Darkness to Eastering

In memoriam: James Coutts (1935–2016)

In gratitude: Stephanie Coutts

'For God is the God who comes, who is always coming towards us.
To go to God, we have to journey by a way that is unfamiliar,
a way that takes us beyond our knowledge.
Yet there is no moment of our day when this God
in Jesus is not coming towards us.'

From Fr Coutts' sermon, Feast of St Anselm, 2016

From Darkness to Eastering

Bonnie B Thurston

wild goose publications

www.ionabooks.com

First published 2017 by
Wild Goose Publications,
21 Carlton Court
Glasgow, G5 9JP, UK
the publishing division of the Iona Community.
Scottish Charity No. SC003794.
Limited Company Reg. No. SC096243.

ISBN 978-1-84952-556-5

Cover image © Ehrlif | Dreamstime.com

The publishers gratefully acknowledge the support of the Drummond Trust,
3 Pitt Terrace, Stirling FK8 2EY in producing this book.

Overseas distribution
Australia: Willow Connection Pty Ltd, Unit 4A, 3-9 Kenneth Road,
Manly Vale, NSW 2093
New Zealand: Pleroma, Higginson Street, Otane 4170, Central Hawkes Bay
Canada: Novalis/Bayard Publishing & Distribution, 10 Lower Spadina Ave.,
Suite 400, Toronto, Ontario M5V 2Z2

Printed by Bell & Bain, Thornliebank, Glasgow

FSC www.fsc.org
MIX
Paper from responsible sources
FSC® C007785

CONTENTS

Holy Week – Transition

Holy Saturday – Waiting

Easter – New Beginning

Eastering – Growth

INTRODUCTION

This is a book about how, on a cosmic and a personal level, darkness gives way to light. It does not sugar-coat the reality of darkness, but examines the ambiguity of growth in darkness, of winter giving way to spring, and growth overcoming frozen stasis. It might not be an entirely cheerful book, but it is a hopeful one because Easter means the light has come, life triumphs, and the promised Holy Spirit will empower us for 'eastering'.

You will find here images of and allusions to Christian scripture and tradition. The frame on which the collection hangs is the movement from Lent through Holy Week to Easter, and beyond it the growth I've called 'eastering'. Some readers will recognise that in making the noun 'Easter' a verbal form ('eastering') I've copied an idea from the final stanza of Gerard Manley Hopkins' extraordinary poem 'The Wreck of the Deutschland'. *'Let him easter in us, be a dayspring to the dimness of us, be a crimson-cresseted east …'* [1] It's a good prayer for any season. Hopkins' poem mirrors (more masterfully than anything you will find herein) the movement from death dealing to eastering that my poems explore.

Since I have introduced Hopkins, let me offer another of his ideas to orient the reader to this book. 'Inscape' is a term Hopkins coined to describe the essential inner nature of a thing, its essence (to use a philosophical term), its 'true nature' or 'true self' (to use more theological ones). Think of it as something like Duns Scotus' 'principle of individuation', which he called *haecceitas* or 'Thisness'. Those who perceive a thing's inscape (see what it is in its most individuated actuality) experience a moment of illumination, an epiphany of sorts (see the poem 'Returning'). I hope this book reveals to you something of the inscape of the passage from death through eastering and beyond.

The Church either wisely coordinated the liturgical seasons with the natural ones or, inevitably, reflected a pattern woven deeply into the design of the creation. There are seasons of utter darkness, aridity, unknowing, ascesis (Lent/winter). They precede times of transition which can be very dramatic (Holy Week, the Triduum), but also involve waiting (Holy Saturday) for the arrival of light, fecundity, fruitfulness, illumination (Easter, 'eastering'). The progression in these poems from Lent to Easter is profoundly Christian, but too mysterious and universally human to be contained by only my tradition, its images and metaphors. It is the archetypal or prototypical movement from darkness to new light, from death to life and, as a result, continued growth. And it is not a once-for-all-time cycle, but one that repeats itself (as the poem 'Easter's Shadow' suggests). While I think this is the 'inscape' of the Christian story, I also think it is one that many people recognise and from which they might draw comfort. If in reading this book such a person meets Jesus Christ Who Incarnated the pattern, was God's gift of making visible the inscape of Being, I would not be disappointed.

That Wild Goose Publications is publishing these poems is a source of great joy. Its readership is exactly the right audience, and for 20 years Iona has taught me about darkness and light. Neil Paynter at Wild Goose is consistently a wonderful, sympathetic editor and e-mail friend. His suggestions have strengthened this collection without obscuring the poet's voice. Esther de Waal has faithfully promoted my poetry and introduced me to Michael Woodward, editor of Three Peaks Press, which brought out my first two slim collections of verse. I am profoundly grateful to them. I am inspired and encouraged by Welsh poets Ruth Bidgood and Anne Cluysenaar (of blessed memory). Closer to home, private readings for Charl and David and electronic consultations with Cheryl and Marc have encouraged my pencil and enhanced my life.

Think of the book as both ticket and passport for a spiritual journey. I remind voyagers who undertake it that 'light shines in the darkness', which I take to mean that darkness is, by design, required to perceive light. The darker it is, the more visible even the tiniest light. According to one of my scientifically knowledgeable friends, the absolute threshold for light is a candle in absolute darkness thirty miles away. For each traveller I pray 'journeying mercies'. And I remind Christian pilgrims, 'Take heart. He will come.'[2]

Bonnie Thurston,
The Anchorage,
Wheeling, WV, USA

1. Gerard Manley Hopkins, *Poems and Prose*, W.H. Gardner (Ed.), Penguin, 1953/1978, p.24
2. From 'Holy Saturday (2)', p.67

Prerequisite

There is devilish danger
in perpetual motion,
consistent clamour.
Stillness precedes awakening:

silence of jet black night
before sweet twitter of birdsong
presages gradual greying,
the rose trumpet of dawn;

slow, perceptible rising
of spring daffodils,
days of stasis before
swollen buds flower;

sterile fallowness
of the unfurrowed heart
before love ploughs through
gloriously furrowing everything.

LENT – DARKNESS

Winter Night/Longest Night

On winter's longest night
ebony stillness unfurls
a field of cosmic sequins
incomparably vast,
flung out sparkling,
granulated from some
mass of stuff
long since exploded.
I ponder galaxies,
each embracing
a hundred billion
shining, spinning suns.

My mind stumbles
in this darkness,
but catches itself
on the solid joy
of living in this galaxy,
whirling around
this little sun,
grateful for firm grasp
of infinitesimal smallness,
expansive as the universe
on winter's longest night.

Dispelling Darkness

Everyone has a shadow side,
a place of interior darkness
against which the heaviest
light-blocking draperies
are carefully drawn,
has corners in which
black mould multiplies.
Ignored, it increases.
Examined, it disperses
like sun's rays refracting
through winter trees.

For most of us darkness
only occasionally leaches
through when it's been
too long since we entered it
armed with a flickering taper.
Sometimes one borrows
another's cleaner light
to cast back the curtains,
and aspirate the spark
that one day might
ignite someone else's.

Winters of the Heart

Life has been
a trudging procession
of frigid weeks.
Many have lumbered by
since it has warmed up
to freezing.

Last night more snow fell,
before a freezing rain.
We awakened
to a crystalline world,
the brittle beauty of ice
like that of dangerous women.

When all is shrouded
in sub-zero pall,
what will melt the ice,
thaw the heart,
assure us that spring
will assert its lovely,
safe self?

Late January

Frigidity and darkness
make the days of winter
after the Star's ascendancy
time to be endured,
gotten through,
survived with such grace
as can be mustered
in a season almost void
of feasts or fecundity.

I shuffle through it,
mentally staggering
under the annual weight
of low grade
but palpable sadness,
heavy as layers of clothing
insulating my body
against piercing cold
that might, in fact, enliven.

The buffers of company
provide no respite.
Who would brave this iciness
to come and call?
Huddled in solitary gloom,
like everything else
I strain to hear
spring's natal command:
'Lazarus! Come out!'

Winter Sunday Morning

There is palpable quietude
this winter Sunday morning,
as if the stillness
calls creation to attend
to some great mystery
hidden behind
appearance's mask.

In my stammering way,
I pray for awakening,
to glimpse colour
in all that is grey,
to hear the song
sung in the depths of life,
to find the joy
wrapped in suffering,
darkness, and obscurity.

Lent in a Russian Novel

The sun begins its descent.
A scattering of rock salt
has eaten small holes,
pockmarked the lane.
Soon it will refreeze
to a glassy mirror
where the waning moon
will admire her face.

Living in this Russian novel,
with windows frozen over,
the enforced solitude
of wearying winter weather
can lead to introspection.
One can accept or reject
its searing invitation
to examine internal fires.

Does God Know?

One doesn't send postcards
when the holiday is spent
staring over the edge
of the abyss
into impenetrable darkness,
into the silence
(not of eternity,
which might be full
of the music of the blessed)
of utter absence.
Who would come here
except by mistake?
Who would come here
except driven by demons?
Does God know?
Is God the equilibrium
which balances on the edge
or the tantalising vertigo
which threatens to plunge
into the chasm of chaos?

The Eye of Despair

Sometimes the best
you can do
is to howl.
When the wound
is so deep
you know the hurt
will never heal,
when the world
is so broken
a universe of prayer
won't repair it,
the best you
can do is howl.

Throw your head back
and (I dare you)
howl like a banshee,
like a she wolf,
like the wild thing
buried in your bones,
and feel rising
from deep, dark places
with the primal power
of your breath
a sliver of hope
to hurl with your howl
at the eye of despair.

Sticking Points

I had worked all morning
on an intractable problem,
a barrier to my project,
had searched the books,
taxed my addled brain,
scratched my empty head,
when close behind me
there was an ominous thud.
I turned to the window.
Two grey wisps of down,
feathery and wavering,
clung to the glass
where some other tiny life
had hit an invisible wall.

Winter Grief

A feeder of sunflower seeds
attracts, not scarlet cardinals,
bluebirds, or indigo buntings,
but chickadees, junkos, titmice,
appropriate decorations
for a decimated season.

The swoop and flutter
of their small, grey lives
dances through deadness,
animates winter trees.
They dare me to hope
that hidden somewhere
in empty branches
buds might be waiting.

Prelude to the Waltz

The rain was prelude
to wet snow which
clung to bud and branch,
muffled night noise,
enforced a frozen stillness.
Nothing moved.

Now the sun rises
behind enfolded hills,
lights the opposite height,
topping the trees with silver
which bejewel the summit,
crown it crystalline.

The lengthening of light
lifts some instinctive baton
that signals recently returned
spring birds to sing,
that gives fair warming
to winter's waning world,

that shatters the witch's
fierce, icy curse,
that, like turning the key
of an animated music box,
recommences the whirling
waltz of time.

March Snow

Great clumps of it
fall from the sky
like somebody up there
is shearing sheep,
or dumping out a duvet,
or throwing cotton balls
at the waiting world.

The absurd, wet snow
of middle March
is laughable, ironic,
a portent of thaw,
a reminder paradox
pervades creation.

Hidden Contours

In winter one sees
otherwise hidden
contours of the land,
how the hills enfold
down the long hollows
providing empty
space for the spring's streams,
how the high ridges
slice the icy sky.

In life's long winter
the contours of life,
age softened and wise,
shyly emerge like
slowly ripened fruit,
a glorious pear,
perhaps slightly bruised,
full of succulent
juice, the shape of hope.

Obeisance

After a long absence,
I found a body
in the library,
first mistook it
for a fallen leaf,
completely desiccated,
perfectly intact,
a small grey carcass,
a dead field mouse.

Things die of absence,
carelessness, inattention,
of wandering into danger
that seemed refuge.
This ritual interment
asks no absolution,
but offers a gesture
of sincere reparation
for my obliviousness.

I kneel in frigid rain
in the muddy garden,
trowel a tiny grave
for the tissue shrouded
corpse in my pocket,
kneel on bad knees
because all life is gift,
worthy of respect
here and hereafter.

Despite Appearances

After desperate deadness
and long, dreadful winter
I was totally seduced
by the tempting tease
of two shining spring days.

One bedraggled crocus,
first in the garden,
bedazzled me before
today's steady rain
turned again to snow.

Something ominous hangs
about the dirty fog
trailing around the hills
like greasy bottle blonde hair
falling on a sloven's shoulders.

Surely beneath all appearances
some vernal beauty awaits
its cue to take centre stage,
in everything something
gives or longs for life.

Winter Turning to Spring

In the saturnine turning
of winter toward spring
there are many thresholds,
doors opening into the void,
false starts, things frozen, stillborn.
Night becomes darker, more viscous,
the cold more penetrating,
everything sapless and hungrier.
Frigid aridity gives lessons in choice,
practice for furious fruitfulness.

We learn full aliveness
in sparseness and scarcity,
and, since everything means,
to choose carefully to what we attend
or are utterly dispersed and distracted
when abundance arrives laughing.
For suddenly, one bright morning,
it will be the fertile season
of sun on silver birches,
of bees in foxglove bells.

Ein Sof*

We scrabble to fill
the world with noise:
relentlessly grinding intellect,
perpetually moving tongue,
electronic racket
our grandparents
couldn't imagine.

If you are quiet,
strive for inner stillness,
waste few words,
many will think you mad.
You will hear within
the vast emptiness
which they fear.

In the beginning, God
created, made everything
from darkness and silence.
What surfaces, emerges
in your empty spaces,
might be a full moon
on your darkest night.

* Ein Sof *is a Kabbalist term meaning 'no limit' or 'infinity'.*

Noche Oscura

The news is occupied
with a perigee moon
and Perseid meteors,
the former only slightly
eclipsing the latter.
The Swift-Tuttle comet
slashes through our
inner solar system,
its trail of dust streaking
fearsome flashes of light.
At 100 meteors an hour,
its fireballs suggest
the sky is, indeed, falling.

I rise in the dark
hours of the morning,
in nightgown and sweater
stumble into the garden
only to stare woozily up
into an overcast sky.
Even the 'super moon'
is partially obscured.
A thick band of cloud
stands sentinel between me
and the beauty of heaven
I nevertheless still hope
might be hidden there.

All These Awakenings

Brightening March collides
with winter temperatures.
In early, bright dawns
even heavy frost, light snow
seem full of promise.

Somewhere spring's first snake
stirs in the brittle skin
it will soon leave behind.
A sleepy mammal stretches
and licks its lustreless fur.

Distant as fleeting memory
the song of a summer bird
echoes through bare trees,
causes vernal vibrations
in my hibernating heart.

All these awakenings
are glorious mysteries.
I stop counting winter beads,
turn again toward the light
at the core of all my longing.

Untimely, Unseemly

Easter is late this year.
Six somber weeks of Lent
are superimposed
on a world laughing
the hilarious joke
of life abundant.

How can I feel penitential,
amused as I am,
by the sap of life rising
to waken the winter world,
to lighten its womb-dark places
with a golden explosion,
a punchline of seed and sun?

Spring in the Valley

Long after day lengthened
winter chill perdured.
Now hellebore blooms.
Daffodils swell to flowering.
Rhubarb's pink, penile head
pushes through nubile soil.
Lilacs burst their buds,
small, purple eruptions of hope.
In the little valley where I live
trees bend toward light,
their odd curvatures
witness to vegetal yearning.
All creation instinctively
leans toward light.
The winter season's stone
rumbles slowly away
from the mouth of life.
In the mind's cave corners
fearsome creatures of darkness
shrink and tremble knowing
their hour, too, has come.

I Can Only Hope

Winter has passed.
I stand barefooted
on fecund earth,
feel its energy,
millions of cells
in my feet meet
millions of cells,
myriad creatures.
Spring's awakening
is retrospective
of the holy grounding
that first framed being.
One day soon earth
will graciously receive
the body I return,
raw material, compost
for the flowering
of other lives with,
I can only hope,
greater joys
than even these.

HOLY WEEK – TRANSITION

Seventh Day

The silence that is
Sunday's renewal
of great mystery
has an odd herald:
dark grey-blue above
the black unfurling
of hill's horizon
a slash of crimson,
bloody serration,
the day's dawn twaining
of heaven and earth.

On the day made for
rest and communion,
this melancholy
separation of
the two creations
is knit together,
illuminated
for a mute watcher
in the deep shadows
by a dying dove
on a barren tree.

Waiting on the Prince of Peace

(On John 16:33)

In the long shadows
of death dealing,
the roiling cities
of prestige and power
where the ego driven
are rewarded
and the humble silenced,
the little carpenter
from nowhere Nazareth,
place from whence
nothing good comes,
bids us be at peace,
satisfied with obscurity,
content to work in darkness
as we wait on dawn
and the king on a donkey.

Palm Sunday, 1979

(B.P., requiescat in pace)

A voice tired of crying out,
A tattered shred of psalm;
There is always the door
Between here and hereafter.
Today you opened it.

What hidden Gethsemani
Did you suffer in hungry darkness?
What private vision of Golgotha
Forced your hand to the ultimate
Gesture of departure?

He chose His destiny
On this day of contradictions
(Promised glory and grave foreboding).
I pray it was for you, too,
An occasion of triumphal entry.

The Heart Is a Field

There is a dormant place
a fallowness in the heart
that awaits awakening,
awaits furrowing,
awaits some seed to be sown
that will take root,
send out tendrils,
fill inner life
with flowers and fruit.

Who will put hand
to that plough, not look back,
ignore stone or weed,
scatter that seed?
Pulsing with potential,
beating beatitude,
the heart is a field.
Who will till and sow
and gather into barns?

Eucharist in a Time of Drought

The kneeler is bare wood.
My knees ache.
I stare through the altar window
at three sere trees.
It is hot, still, silent as death.

Then, ever so gently,
just at the threshold of sound,
a whisper of rain,
a tentative, shy rustling
like the murmur
of familiar, holy words.

It is the sound of life,
heaven breaking open,
pouring promise
on the dry ground,
the holy ground,
of drought-stricken hearts.

Politics in Holy Week

Centuries change;
the dynamics are
remarkably consistent.
The political questions remain:
Who has power?
Who gives it?

Some assert
authority of office,
forgetting their fragility,
inflate ego like balloons
at a children's party.

Few (but some)
do unselfing's bitter work,
know the universal centre
is elsewhere,
exhibit integrity's authority.

The swagger of armies,
posturing of princes,
prelates, presidents,
pale before the power
of the little Jewish teacher
from phyletic Palestine.

Wenn Kömmt das Schöne

Not eating,
a small downy woodpecker
clings to the cage
holding a block of suet,
her striped head
cocked intelligently
toward the kitchen window
behind which I stand
not washing dishes,
also listening.
Bach BWV 82:
Ich Habe Genug:
'Mein Gott! Wenn kömmt
das schöne: Nun!'

Deadheading

Deadheading daffodils
is sad, but necessary work.
When the rich, yellow trumpet
goes all papery and transparent
it begins to draw life
from the bulb which stores it
for next year's flowering.
So, like a minor executioner,
I lop off heads – snip, snip, snip –
watch them fall haphazardly
to the gentler earth
which gathers up old life
to make it new again.

Outside Carmel's Chapel Window

I watch slow-budding
trees unfurling spring's
most fragile leaves.
It puts me in
mind of seed sending
down roots before
breaking through
soil into sun,
silently bespeaking
hidden activity of One
Who clothes the lilies
of the field,
knows the birds
of the air,
Who is their song
and the ears
that hear it,
Who brings to birth
and bids us die
to feed like seed
a world that neither
knows nor cares
that we are rooted
in life's loam,
daily proffer the fruit
of death's demise.

Sutton's Warbler, Unconfirmed Sighting

Unlike pudgy chickadees
with whom it shared the feeder,
this bird had a peculiar beauty,
an elegant, sleek body,
daffodil yellow throat,
grey coat over snowy shirt,
kohl under, white shadow
above its tiny, avian eyes.
It even ate delicately,
singularly, without mate
or observable companion.
Yes, I know. It is a rarity.
Peterson says 'not expected'.
This may be the wrong place,
and I am no ornithologist.
Officialdom didn't recognise
the Son of God either.
But the *laoi* knew
what they had seen.

Life-sized Stations

On the grey gravelled road
to the sisters' cemetery
are life-sized stations of the cross,
white concrete and stark
against their evergreen background.

This morning a little girl
in a frilly skirt with flounces,
a lady (probably her mother)
in dark slacks, a red blouse
were stopping at each.

They stood together looking.
The lady sometimes gestured,
spoke to the child who, apparently
happily, skipped, arms swinging,
from station to station.

When clear, spring mornings
of childhood are long past,
the small girl is herself a woman,
how will she remember the day
her mother introduced the Via Crucis?

Fiat

There comes from nowhere
with no connection
to the present moment
or circumstance
a wave of sadness
abrupt and acute
as a paper cut,
making eyes tear,
the breath tense,
as if a telegram brought
some terrible news,
or a phone call
announced a tragedy.

This momentary mourning
is unmoored, unrelated
to personal circumstance,
one's pain, perplexity,
slings and arrows.
It is life's great
free-floating sorrow,
the desperate keening
of a broken world,
its unborn dying,
its causeless martyrs,
all that suffers alone
and unlamented.

Perhaps aspiring
to soothe the universe,
one can accept it simply,
live it secretly,
this mysterious vocation
to help God bear
unimaginable burdens.
Unlike conscripted
Simon of Cyrene,
one can voluntarily
carry this concealed cross
and, trembling, trudge
toward resurrection.

The Nails

In the convent guest house
a crucifix hung over the bed,
but it was slightly askew.

The Corpus leaned off it,
arms extended like Zorba,
or a dervish warming up to whirl.

My mind did not embrace
crucifixion as cosmic dance.
I tried to straighten it, but
the nail was driven crookedly.

No one controls the cross.
In its extraordinary dance
everything depends
upon the nails.

No Ambiguity

Occasionally I hear that sort
of thumping, literal-minded
preaching on evening radio,
or swipe metaphorically
at sticky arachnoid words
spun darkly from the Web,
dangerous as broken bottles
set in cement atop a wall
of unshakeable certainties.

Into that black and white world
Jesus shines heaven's grey glory,
offers the wavering doubtful
not a condemnatory screed,
but beguiling invitation,
reaches down with bloodied hands
that breached walls, broke barriers,
gladly shepherds poor, wobbly
us, hopeless illiteralists,
toward the divine reality:
His unambiguously riven side.

Sitting with Sorrow

Though perhaps untapped
every life retains
subterranean streams
of living water.
Any sadness not kept at bay
but accepted or embraced
touches the deepest sorrow,
reaches hidden griefs,
the heart's unhealed
bruises and brokenness.

This makes weeping
a sacrament of hope.

Tears are the rising
of internal waters,
proof one is not
yet so desiccated
as to turn from or forget
other's sufferings
which are the unity
in the world's patchwork,
which are the pattern
in its randomness.

Whiteout

Not so long ago
out on the prairie,
Hazel Miner was entrusted
with her little brother and sister.
The darkening day bespoke
the coming blizzard.
School closed at noon.
They headed home
in a horse-drawn sleigh.
Lost in a white night,
Hazel tucked her siblings in
beneath her own body,
waited for help that came
the next day and found
her dead, the others safe.
Did the little ones
know in the clear
if inarticulate way
of wisdom's children
the anguish of hope,
that in giving it away
one imparts the power
of indestructible life?

Altar of Repose

The solemn stripping past,
incense extinguished,
music stilled,
the Lord is entombed
on a barren altar,
and we, the gathered
remnant, watch.

This arid, memorial night
I remember wilderness
where Satan, that twisted elf,
tempted Jesus to make
bread from stone.
At table this desert night
with beloved and betrayer
He trumped the tempter
and made bread God
before Whom we kneel
immersed in adoration,
plunged deep in dense,
severe and tender joy.

Though the darkness deepens,
somewhere God remains.
Like Mary of Magdala
in the garden of crucifixion,
we wait opposite His tomb,
keeping vigil, listening
for the Shepherd's voice.

Transitus

The obituary page
of any local paper
lists a spate of funerals
following big holidays.
People live toward
future joys, perish
from hopelessness.

Coming to a kindly end,
the elderly and ill
are apt to die,
not at witching time,
or in the wee hours
after darkest midnight,
but nearer morning.

Brother Death lurks
close to the light,
within sight of dawn
which offers some
secret summons
to depart before it arrives,
to cross to the Other Shore
and the Greater Light
in which, we dare to hope,
there is no darkness at all.

Tenebrae

Oblivious to the outside world,
we drop our lamentations
into utter darkness,
chant cries to Jerusalem,
calls to return,
sing haunted antiphons,
then kneel in silence.

Outside the church,
out beyond humanity's
long night watch,
a lone bird warbles.
Regardless of us,
in the selfless east,
the sun slowly rises.

HOLY SATURDAY – WAITING

Transformation

There is a crossing over
from which there is no return.
It can be chosen,
or you may find yourself
on the other side
not knowing how
your *transitus* occurred.

You may remain
in the same place,
dwell among the same people,
but all is forever changed.
What was can never be again.
What will be is shrouded
in a fog of unknowing.

Removed from the roots
that bound and fed you,
the soil has fallen away.
You cannot go back,
the earth has closed.
There is only empty air,
the waiting and the hope.

In Our Own Image

It has never been just,
but more than what passes
for love among us.
We cannot cope with
its wild unpredictability,
over millennia tried to tame
its seasons with our colours –
purple, green, red,
most mysterious, white –
tame its worship with words,
contain its pervasive presence
in attractive edifices,
put it in a golden box
set in a stone wall
lit by a crimson candle,
with archaic ceremony,
weekly take it out,
nibble a tiny bit,
go home satisfied,
unaware we consumed
a seed of something shattering.
Should it sprout within,
we quickly weed it out
of our carefully maintained
and cultivated gardens,
preferring to make idols
in our own image than
to adore its fierce fecundity.

None of this works.
It remains unruly
and incomprehensible.
But those who listen
into their most authentic
unknowing might hear
its irrepressible laughter
and be comforted.

Waiting

Dogs – a pack of them –
scruffy, mud-coloured,
medium-sized mutts,
thoroughly disreputable,
wait outside the door's
unreflecting mirror.

Snouts sniffing,
some wagging,
tails thumping,
two humping,
most just sit there.

I, too, do it endlessly.
The next stage
is essentially unimportant.
Grovelling cur,
I am absurdly grateful
when allowed to proceed.

It is not the waiting
but the unknowing
that drags the old,
wet rug of time
across my living room.

A dog, utterly mongrel,
I am not patience incarnate.
A foolish, sleeping virgin,
I do not know the day or hour
when the bridegroom will arrive,
but he, like everything, is long expected.

'... I Will Give You Rest'

After the suffering,
before the shouts,
this is the startling gift:
Holy Saturday, the garden
in the place of crucifixion.
Here the stone of silence
is rolled against the tomb
of talk and trivialisation.
Here chant and cant
of church is stilled.
Here the world waits
with nothing to do
but listen into mystery,
embrace the darkness
of profound unknowing,
watch toward inky east.

Holy Saturday (1)

After the night of tears,
the noon of darkness,
a whole day's space,
the seventh day,
the day God rested
from making,
from being un-made.

Christ has died.
Life is hidden
in God's obscurity.
Adam lay ybounden
with fruitless Eve.
Nobody can be sure
what will happen next.

I love this day
of silent waiting
when fasting is over,
feasting not begun,
when pain is past
but flesh not quickened.
This is where we live,

this human space,
waiting before the cave
in the tarnished garden
where it all began
and ended
to begin anew,
we hope, forever.

Holy Saturday, Early Spring

'All the trees of the wood shall shout for joy
before the Lord when he comes.' (Psalm 96:12b–13a)

But it has not happened yet.
The festal shout
is but feathery potential.
The forest face is veiled in lace,
the mauve, burgundy, green
tipping not yet leafing branches.
One almost hears the cry
in the orchard's pink *pianissimo*,
enormous chorus of swollen blossoms
singing of fruit to be.

The forest orchestra is tuned,
waiting in electric silence
for the conductor
to take up his baton,
signal the stone splitting crescendo,
the triumphant opening chord,
and creation's groaning
bondage to decay
becomes symphonic celebration,
an aria of risen-ness and life.

Holy Saturday (2)

It was raw and cold,
no hint of resurrection.
Driving to friends
on a winter scarred road,
under lowering pines,
I saw a great patch
(more than I'd ever
seen before)
of snowdrops,
Samuel Arnott's,
spring's first flowers.
'Take heart,' they said.
'He will come.'

Holy Saturday Vespers

At the end of a day of wind
tossing cloud and sun
back and forth behind
the unclothed trees,
now, in late afternoon,
light comes in wavering shafts
into the monastic garden.
Since yesterday, crocus opened.
On the intricate witch hazel
swollen, crimson buds
have become featheriest
of yellow-green leaves.
Even mysteriously lovely,
death-dealing hellebore
are illuminated by ribbons
of anodyne light.
This coming night
tames all wild darkness,
makes it the place
we meet and dwell
within Him in Whom
there is none at all.

Crown of Life

Long before they crown,
deep within our bodies
our children develop
senses they do not need
in the safety of the womb,
but that will wound
and heal their lives here.

Suppose this life
is womb of another,
that death's dark passage
is a birth canal.
How does this body
prepare for another?
What sensibilities
need nourishing now
for the crowning
of that unseen then?

Time Lapse

Sometimes in autumn
when dying is so lovely,
or in succulent spring
when life returns
with wild abandon
and speaks one's name
causing breath to catch
between chest and throat,
one has a fleeting sense
of standing fragile
on the very edge
of all humanity
might remember,
a sense of vertigo
as if all the past
might topple off
beyond the present,
and our so carefully
guarded secrets
flutter like falling leaves
into forgotten futures.

The Harrowing of Hell

' … mercy triumphs over judgement' (James 2:13)

In the icons, Jesus
victoriously straddles
a gaping darkness,
firmly grasps
by their pale hands
Adam and Eve,
like the carnival
strongman who sounds
the bell with his blow,
exultantly pulls them
from shattered sepulchres.

But before all this
there must have been
a great assize, separation
of sheep from goats.
Hell was populated,
peopled with the judged
(like our ancient parents).
Prior justice carried out
in some cosmic courtroom
was now completed
as mercy drew it
blinking uncomprehendingly,
triumphantly forth
from darkness and death.

Before the Empty Tabernacle

Little wonder the women
went to the tomb.
We seek those we knew
in places we knew them,
places they had been,
places where we put them.
But, in spite of us, our
beloved leave, change,
go elsewhere or
are seemingly absent
until we are able to look
in unexpected places,
see them in least likely faces,
allow the truth
of the imperfect past
to nudge us into
the unimagined future.

Easter Vigil

After the sun sank, gold and crimson,
after the elevation of primal elements –
new fire, water, evergreen branch –
after the bells and the first feast,
after we broke our fast from alleluia,
we dispersed into a soft, spring night
under a sky resplendent with stars,
but absent of the full, bright moon.

Later, from sweet sleep of Easter's first wine,
I was awakened by silent luminescence.
In an unfamiliar corner of the sky
the milky, radiant moon hung in the trees,
beautiful and dignified, unearthly power,
as the lesser light gave way to the greater,
as deepest night knelt before this dawn.

First Light

Easter feast's first light
occurs outside church,
a fire we build
in the parking lot,
carry with singing
into the church's
obscure, dark cavern
soon awash with words
about mysteries which
are unspeakable.

Much later I stand
mute, awestruck beneath
'the moon and stars
which Thou hast made',
smell in spring's wet earth
Easter day's first light
silently creeping
over hill and field,
just as Christ's rising,
forever's first dawn,
blossoming outside
the church's confines.

EASTER – NEW BEGINNING

The Third Day

Dead grass erupted
through dirty snow
in grey, scrofulous patches
as, day before yesterday,
fog the colour of dirty dishwater
fell like a dark curtain
in an isolation ward,
imprisoning the world
in a nightmare
of dissolution and ooze.

Yesterday, heavy, wet snow
covered those horrors
in yards of misshapen cotton wool.
Although early morning
other creatures had precedence.
Deer, birds, a rabbit,
something ominously feline
left their tracks before the sun
rose in blinding revelation
of life's connectedness.

On this, the third day,
the merest of appearances:
the tips of daffodils
roll back stones,
take a tentative peek
from the frozen grave.
In astonished stillness,
everything holds its breath,

waiting to see
what will happen next.

Easter Morning, Before Dawn

Driving out the ridge
before the horizon
is crimson-cresseted,
my route is bisected
by a late bat wobbling
back to barn or belfry.
It startles an early owl
prowling for its small,
unfortunate breakfast.

Over my left shoulder
just past its fullness,
the misshapen moon
is shyly suspended
behind a latticework
of unleaved trees.

A comfortable companion,
this lesser of two great lights.
Still, it rules night and stars,
fulfils a divine mandate
to separate the darkness,
give light upon earth,
determine ocean's tides.
It alleviates nocturnal
solitude, leads me home.

Lent's Requiem

Marked with ashes,
all this dark winter
we were shrouded
in purple,
royal colour,
colour of penitence.

One sad Friday
even that was taken.
The altar of our hearts
stripped, colourless, bare,
we waited
in silence, darkness.

Wearing purple wounds,
crowned with spring,
Christ came quickly.
The gracious Grave Robber
took the tomb's treasure,
stole the sting of death,
once and for all
scattering the shrouds
in the illumination
of His Heart.

Easter Sunday Morning

Not one of them, I don't object
to Christmas and Easter Christians,
hope they are welcomed and return.
But I have begun to stay home.
Amid the noise and pageantry
I lose track of the mystery
rising like tiny spring irises,
purple, this year silent through snow.
For me, finches in the feeder,
the sweet, wet smell of waking soil,
quiet, even cloudy, dawning
are alleluia and incense,
candle, choir, sermon enough.
Still, I listen to hear my name
spoken in an empty garden
from which angels have departed.
With Magdalene, I watch and wait.

Why Are You Weeping?

Mary stood weeping
not knowing where.
She last saw him alive
framed by thieves.
With tear smeared eyes,
fuzziness of great grief,
she bends to the tomb
she'd seen sealed,
experiences the shock
of empty space
between two angels,
then turns toward
the Unrecognised,
His flesh untabernacled,
soon to ascend,
be the vibrant void
pulsing above two
gold winged cherubim,
the living mercy seat.
But first
    He speaks her name.

The Stone

The Myrrh Bearers came
(with what fear and trembling?)
trudging alone in darkness
worrying about
the stone.

Everybody worries about
the stone,
that great impediment
between us
and what we seek,

the great burden
we carry
like Sisyphus
labouring
up and down the hill.

The sun rose.
The women looked up.
The stone,
which was very large,
had been removed.

No wonder they ran
to tell Cephas.
Somebody should tell Sisyphus:
'Put it down, man,
and dance on it.'

Holy Sepulchre/Church of the Resurrection

With its mud brown walls
no one could call it
a beautiful church.
(No gold dome, no blue tiles.)

Constantine first built it
over a broken rock,
over a gallows,
over a tomb.

A once fine basilica
was carved up by Crusaders.
Ecclesiastical hierocrats
continue the subdivision.

It houses a collection
of bad religious art,
harbours the crassest of tourists
and their lying guides.

It's cluttered,
noisy and dirty,
embracing as it does
the hollow, harried, holy.

This is holy ground,
the soul's *omphalos*,
as sacred as it gets
in this veil of tears.

Here God emptied Himself.
Good to the last drop
of His precious blood,
here God died.

God's mother saw it,
the lance, water, blood,
the broken body of her Son:
dead, dead, dead.

Here God emptied Himself
so completely
that life could rush in.
God emptied Himself alive.

Death gave birth to life.
Here life won
once and for all.
No wonder the rock split.

Who can imagine the energy
that empowered a tomb
to swallow a cross
and spit out God?

No one could call it
a beautiful church,
but God emptied Himself alive
here, once, for all.

Glass

One reads extraordinary things
in ordinary magazines.
I am arrested by the knowledge
glass, that 3,500-year-old gift,
is neither solid, liquid, nor gas.
What lets in the light,
contains the proffered water,
is of indeterminate state,
incarnate, but not matter
in its normal configurations.

The article says glass is liquid,
frozen in an unstable state.
I do not understand this,
how glass can thus exist.
Oddly, it gives me insight
into Christ's *morphe*: God
incarnate; form: incomprehensible.
'Liquid solidified in unstable state'
also elucidates why sometimes
brokenness manifests such holiness.

In the Eastering Cosmos

The universe gasped,
held its breath from Friday
until this moment's exhale,
a cosmic expansion
sending ripples
through the fabric of space.

We perceive sequentially,
but there is only now.
There are infinite numbers
of ways to be bent,
but only one to be flat;
so there is an infinite
catalogue of deadness,
only one way to life.

The stone may have rolled
of its own volition.
Nothing is completely
inert or inanimate.
Everything pulses energy.
Even rocks long for life.

Testimony

I left the garden aeons ago
taking only the sweat of my brow
and knowledge of my guilt.

I had been long barren,
heard no laughter,
had no sons like stars to fill heaven.

I had carried my sacrifice
to within sight of the place,
but the bushes yielded neither ram nor fire.

I have risen and fallen like the Nile,
seen swarms of locusts,
repeatedly lost the firstborn.

I wandered forty years in the wilderness
waiting for stones to become bread
and water to flow from the rocks.

The enemy had marched around my city,
broken its walls, defiled its temple,
carried off its riches.

I sat under a gourd tree,
but saw no visions,
no flesh in the valley of dry bones.

I had pulled a thousand buckets
from the village well,
but no kind stranger ever spoke.

By the time I reached Emmaus,
I no longer expected
a travelling companion.

But gracious time trimmed my lamp.
For me, who had no dowry,
a bridegroom waited.

He walked beside me.
The dove descended.
Wine flowed from water jugs.

Easter's Shadow

A shadow passes over.
In windy prelude
to warm spring rain
petals careen
from crab apple trees,
blow like snow
in wild, fragrant exuberance.
An explosion of blossoms
signals life returned.

The cosmic grain of wheat
has fallen and died.
That death is requisite
for all this flowering
is the passing shadow
of impenetrable mystery.
Hidden in the lilies
is a darkness
to be left undisturbed.

EASTERING – GROWTH

General Resurrection

Ancient church cemeteries
planted their people
feet toward the east,
toward the rising sun,
toward Christ's return,
ready to see first
his luminous face,
ready to leap into
his fiery embrace.

From friendly ground
long lovingly tended,
I imagine them
all rising as one,
unidirectional,
undivided in intent,
a great multitude
marching together
toward the unimaginable.

Demythologising

It was bad enough
that He kicked the dog
at the door of Hades.
Now He's gone
and put Charon
out of business.

He brings folk
from both sides
of the Styx
together,
invites them all
to gather for suppers
He hosts around
His Father's table.

Plant Parable

I do not know
What possessed me,
Why I continued
To water dead stalks.

When leaves began to wither,
I tried to avoid catastrophe,
Manipulated light, added
A variety of synthetic foods.

But I could not reverse
The inevitable progression.
The last leaves fell,
Victims of an open window.

Yet I watered dry earth.
Did I know instinctively
The soil was rich and fertile?
Was some deeper reverence at work?

Imagine my surprise
When, during the night,
The corpse sprouted
Two brilliant green leaves.

Veriditas

Long before it is visible
one hears the greening
in spring birdsong,
in drilling woodpecker,
smells it in thaw-perfumed
softening wind, ripe
with luscious, living loam.
Snowdrops lead crocuses
which slowly emerge
like vegetable gemstones,
and hellebore heads droop
dangerous, purple beauty.
Late March snow doesn't
long delay its dawning.
On brittle branch
palest green bud
teases the very tip
of a frozen life
which might be yours.

Resurrection

After a winter of heavy snow,
in a dirty early spring,
the lamentable extent
of broken trees is visible.
Today in one
sun-warmed place
not grass, but crocuses,
a whole hillside
of Lenten purple,
Easter golden ones
by their muddy triumph
are singing spring.

Early rising, exuberant
expressions of life
invite me to listen
so deeply that I hear
each waking thing
singing in its own voice
for the singular reason
that, in fact, it can,
was made for peculiar
melody. Thus each
soloist eventually
achieves choral spring.

Spring Psalm

Only at this season
do we enjoy forsythia's
golden explosion
or tulips' full palette.
Only at this season
are fields so emerald,
their architecture so clear,
trees having not yet leafed
and obscured earth's
imagined corners.
If my eyes could sing
they would make of
this *veriditas* doxology,
as would my tongue
touched with good wine,
or my fingers skimming
the perfection of your skin.
No created beauty is
too insignificant to adore,
too small for us to psalm.

Cosmic Potlatch

'The heavens declare the glory of God;
the firmament shows God's handiwork.' (Psalm 19:1)

Well, yes, especially now
in the full fury of spring
with apple trees in bloom,
wind blowing petal pink snow,
blinding whiteness of dogwood
against violet speckled verdancy
of winter wakened fields,
when torrential beauty pours
from soon-to-clear skies
leaving the world washed, shiny.

Spring is a cosmic potlatch
amassing all that's beautiful
precisely to give it away
in the annual gesture of generosity,
gracious proof that
it's possible to begin again.

Like Grass of the Field

Don't sit this one out.
This life is the only chance
we get to dance
at creation's wedding feast.

God's cotillion
flings open doors
for everybody.
Indulge the Precious Five!

Everything we know
bodily is holy.
Every body we meet
is a dancing partner

who goes the way of all flesh.
Like the grass of the field,
we might as well dance
when the wind blows a waltz.

Steeplechase

The hurdle comes
hurtling toward us
faster, it seems,
as it approaches,
and higher,
bars rising
of their own accord,
framed by bushes
and a water trench
Elijah on Carmel
would have coveted
for prophets of Baal.

Neither I nor
my little pony
stand a chance
of clearing it
as we thunder on.
Why spur him on,
not rein him in?
Because it is too late
to do anything but soar,
land triumphantly
in an explosion of turf,
heart still pounding
with the wonder of it.

Ticket to Eternity

Only in this moment,
in complete attention,
in being fully here
does eternity exist.
Any tiny thing
can be the now
that breaks enslavement
to linear, limiting time.

Have you really seen
the first crocus
struggled up through snow,
small and slightly bruised
but golden as summer?
Look. It is your ticket
to eternity, resurrection
in your muddy garden.

Returning

'... in returning and rest ye shall be saved ...' (Isaiah 30:15b)

Perhaps not immutable,
place is inexhaustible.
Returning to known ones
does not diminish them
or make them go dark,
but more luminous.
One sees what shines
through the surfaces,
notices more deeply details
that are the pulse of place.
Returning, one migrates
from large to small,
attends to minutest things,
passes into place's infinity.

By Design Seasonal

One might wish to save
this perfect spring day
against the darkness
and death of winter,
somehow preserve
spring's green palette,
its white to yellow gold,
it pink to crimson,
seen in clarity of light
undimmed by summer haze.
But life, by design,
is seasonal, its joys
found in being present,
awake where we are.

Tropicana

An almost vulgarly
showy species of rose,
on this solitary, still,
early Sunday morning
it sings three perfect
orangey-pink flowers,
a trinity of joy
on which dark acolyte
eyes of the other flora
gaze in adoration.

Planted early spring
after the beloved's
slow, bitter demise,
it has endured
ravenous deer,
frigid winters,
inexpert transplantation,
and, like the love
it memorialises,
survived, blossoms.

Having Glimpsed

(On the Feast of St Isidore)

A year of unseasonable weather
cleaning ditch lines, raking leaves
rather than shovelling snow in January.

The snow came in Holy Week,
pelted down Easter Sunday,
nipped first garden growth.

Such desultory thoughts float through
as I cut dead canes from climbing roses
which, damaged, did not die.

I treasure this tiny seed of joy,
knowing that, however minutely,
nature always turns toward life.

Still, no gardener likes pruning,
finds it counter-intuitive to cut
rather than to cultivate.

But such severities bring growth.
New leaves inhabit spaces made
when the weak or dead is removed.

In this process I, too, get cut,
bleed off life's dead ends,
wait for buds to fill empty places.

In the Seeing

In the quiet solitude
of winter darkness and snow
I ponder of what dusty stuff
human holiness might be made.

Is it in the seeing,
light's lengthening,
growing brighter, coming
finally to full sight?

In spring I see
half a dozen goldfinches
flutter a brilliant helix
around a tube of thistle seed,

a pair of Monarch butterflies
in deep purple lilac cones,
crab apple's three glory days,
blooming and letting go,

in spring's slow greening,
apparent randomness of time,
glimpse a unity, pattern
in a patchwork world.

Interpretation of Tongues

Quietly, quietly do you call,
speak in the most ordinary
and exquisite things:
somnambulant silence of snow;
crashing chord of spring's
sudden, symphonic opening;
trill of summer warbler;
barely perceptible rustle
of autumnal leaf loss.
Your basso quavers
in commonplace arias.

Hidden or unbidden
there is nothing
that does not contain you,
nowhere your voice
is completely silenced.
Yours is a language
of profound beauty,
one we no longer speak.
But a few hoary scholars
still translate your tongues.
So much depends on the few.

Spring Sunday Morning Psalm

Benedicite, Omnia Opera Domini

Dawn warblers trill matins.
Three fragile does,
two thin and raggedy,
one larger, sleeker,
survivors of severe winter,
limp across the hill
this fresh, fecund day.
Chipmunks skitter about
on their voracious business
of petty larceny.
The field is darkened
by a murder of crows,
the feeder enlightened
by a charm of goldfinches,
lemon yellow against
a greening world.
Woodpecker's tattoo
thunders the sermon.
Beloved noxious weed,
wild multiflora roses
require no thurifer
to dispense incense.

And – oh gift of wonder! –
well-hidden in
sun splotched woods,
a patch of forget-me-nots
offers shy azure prayer.
This is my church,
the congregation
to which I most
worshipfully belong.
Here I praise and
magnify you forever –
or at least until
doves coo compline
and darkness closes in.

Dust to Dust

Our life's pilgrimage
is unicursal.
There might be seasons
of long wandering,
or time traversing
a verdant valley,
rest by still waters,
a hard ascending
of forbidding heights,
or diversions down
dreadful dead ends.
Yet the path remains,
perhaps obscure, but
universally
one directional.
In the eternal
human procession
each one's journey winds
to a gaping grave.
Each person is a
one way street toward
the matter from which
they were constructed,
the stuff under foot
into which God breathed,
will again breathe, life.

Better

Because the very last
wisp of smoke
can be perfect prayer,
total submission,
sometimes it is better
not to rekindle fire,
better not to blow
on embers in the ashes,
better to acquiesce
to inevitable demise
of flickering light,
better not to fear
the darkness.

Acknowledgements

'Winter Night/Longest Night' – *Winter: Liturgical resources for November, December and January,* Ruth Burgess, Wild Goose Publications, 2016

'The Eye of Despair' – *The Merton Journal* (17/1, 2010)

'Waiting on the Prince of Peace' – *We Will Seek Peace and Pursue It: Reflections and prayers for peace and reconciliation,* Neil Paynter (Ed.), Wild Goose Publications, 2015

'Deadheading' – *Review for Religious* (68/3, 2009)

'Fiat' – *Weavings* (30/2, 2015)

'Altar of Repose' – *Spirituality* (22/125, March-April, 2016)

'Tenebrae' – The Sun Slowly Rises: Readings, reflections and prayers for Holy Week from the Iona Community, Neil Paynter (Ed.), Wild Goose Publications, 2017

'... I Will Give You Rest' – *Spirituality* (22/125, March-April, 2016)

'Holy Saturday (1)' – *Hints and Glimpses,* Bonnie B Thurston, Three Peaks Press, Abergavenny, Wales, 2004

'Holy Saturday, Early Spring' – *Hints and Glimpses,* Bonnie B Thurston, Three Peaks Press, Abergavenny, Wales, 2004

'Holy Saturday Vespers' – *Spirituality* (22/125, March-April, 2016)

'The Harrowing of Hell' – *The Sun Slowly Rises: Readings, reflections and prayers for Holy Week from the Iona Community,* Neil Paynter (Ed.), Wild Goose Publications, 2017

'Before the Empty Tabernacle' – *Spirituality* (22/125, March-April, 2016)

'Easter Vigil' – *The Dayspring* (106/1, 2007)

'First Light' – *The Sun Slowly Rises: Readings, reflections and prayers for Holy Week from the Iona Community*, Neil Paynter (Ed.), Wild Goose Publications, 2017

'Lent's Requiem' – *The Dayspring* (99/2, 2000)

'Why Are You Weeping?' – *Spirituality* (22/125, March-April, 2016)

'The Stone' – *Practicing Silence: New and selected verse*, Bonnie Thurston, Paraclete Press, 2014

'Holy Sepulchre/Church of the Resurrection' – *The Chronicle of St George's College*, Spring 2001

'Plant Parable' – *Hill and Valley* (3/5, 1980)

'Dust to Dust' – *The Sun Slowly Rises: Readings, reflections and prayers for Holy Week from the Iona Community*, Neil Paynter (Ed.), Wild Goose Publications, 2017

Wild Goose Publications, the publishing house of the Iona Community established in the Celtic Christian tradition of Saint Columba, produces books, e-books, CDs and digital downloads on:

- holistic spirituality
- social justice
- political and peace issues
- healing
- innovative approaches to worship
- song in worship, including the work of the Wild Goose Resource Group
- material for meditation and reflection

For more information:

Wild Goose Publications
The Iona Community
21 Carlton Court, Glasgow, G5 9JP, UK

Tel. +44 (0)141 429 7281
e-mail: admin@ionabooks.com

or visit our website at
www.ionabooks.com
for details of all our products and online sales